Some Answers Concerning Predestination and Free Will
ELECTION, REJECTION, WHOSOEVER

M.E. JACOB

WESTBOW
PRESS®
A DIVISION OF THOMAS NELSON
& ZONDERVAN

WestBow Press books may be ordered through booksellers or by contacting:

WestBow Press
A Division of Thomas Nelson & Zondervan
1663 Liberty Drive
Bloomington, IN 47403
www.westbowpress.com
844-714-3454

Scripture quotations are taken from the Holy Bible,
King James Version. (Public Domain)

ISBN: 978-1-6642-9273-4 (sc)
ISBN: 978-1-6642-9272-7 (e)

Library of Congress Control Number: 2023903083

Print information available on the last page.

WestBow Press rev. date: 03/01/2023

To my Lord and Savior,
Yeshua Hamashiach, (Jesus is Lord)

Ayn Rand
"Contradictions do not exist. Whenever you think that you are facing a contradiction, check your premises. You will find that one of them is wrong."

If free will means, free will, then are our assumptions concerning predestination correct?

Romans 11:25 For I would not, brethren, that ye should be ignorant of this mystery, lest ye should be wise in your own conceits, that a blindness in part is happened to Israel, until the fulness of the Gentiles be come in. 26 And so all Israel shall be saved: as it is written, There shall come out of Sion the Deliverer,, and shall turn away ungodliness from Jacob:

(The above mentioned Jacob, is not the individual, but the blinded/hardened part of Israel).

CONTENTS

PREDESTINATION AND FREE WILL RECONCILED THROUGH THE MYSTERY OF THE HARDENING OF PART OF ISRAEL, REVEALED IN CHRIST JESUS

DEFINING SCRIPTURE BY SCRIPTURE

The necessity of this book comes for three main reasons:

1. To edify and bring unity in The Church
2. God is a God of peace and not confusion (1 Cor. 14:33 For God is not a God of confusion but of peace.)
3. Moving The Church from a balanced theology into a full reconciliation of predestination and free will.

Within the pages of this book, one will not find a "rehashing" of the tired old positions of the pure predestination position or the pure free will position. You will not find the man made constructs of "life as a canvas", and you will not be told that you cannot understand God and will not understand Him until you get to heaven. What will be discussed is that we can understand God in the person of Jesus Christ. We will also see, through the laying out of scripture, that predestination and free will can be fully reconciled through the understanding of The Mystery of the Blindness/Hardening of a Part of Israel. This Mystery revealed in Christ, is multifaceted so the aspects will be laid out, only using scripture to define scripture for one to see the whole picture.

One must always trust in the Holy Spirit to lead us in all understanding, no matter how long it takes. When we make the love of God and Christ, the umpire of all of our studies of God and His Character, He will lead us to the truth.

Let us now see how free will, can indeed, be fully reconciled with the predestined elect, through the thorough understanding of the mystery of the hardening of part of Israel. Again, scripture will only be defined by scripture. Scripture will be systematically laid out to tell this story.

Within the pages of this book, you will find a total and complete support of the prevailing theme of God's grace which can be summed up in John 3:16

John 3:16 For God so loved the world, that he gave his only begotten Son, that whosoever believeth in him should not perish, but have everlasting life. 17 For God sent not his Son into the world to condemn the world; but that the world through him might be saved.

Man's free will and the angel's free will, operate only within the parameters of God's PURPOSE.

I do not support the misunderstanding of election, that would in essence change the meaning of the above scripture to read something like: for God so loved his elect, that he sent his Son, and everyone else is totally depraved and are vessels, destined to perish. Please define for yourself in Hebrew and Greek, the definitions of hell and wrath. Wrath is not hell. I also do not support that there is only God's will at work in our world because that would mean that God is sinning against himself. In God and Christ, there is no sin and they cannot sin. God is a thrice Holy God and cannot sin and does not sin against Himself. Christ is God, (part of the Trinity), and is/was sinless. Christ is the only person that was ever sinless. Christ did not sin, and God cannot sin. With all of the evil and sin in the world, we must not misunderstand this point. God is indeed Sovereign in the Universe, however the free will of angels and man exists within His Universe and do not negate His Sovereignty. We must not confuse God's Sovereignty, with God's Sovereign PURPOSEFUL DESIGN of our world.

As I stated before, the free will of mankind and the free will of angels, exist only within the parameters of God's purpose.

I hope if you struggling with this subject, and how to reconcile free will and election, you will read on.

ACKNOWLEDGEMENTS

I am grateful to the love of my heavenly Father and my earthly father, Paul, to where I could believe in love to be my guide in life and the writing of this book. I am grateful to the Holy Spirit, to bring to remembrance scripture. I am grateful to the grace of my Lord, Yeshua (Jesus). I am grateful to the faith of my mother, Marie, that taught me that God can do exceedingly, abundantly above all that I ask or think. I am grateful to my husband Don, for supporting me through this walk. I am grateful for the love of my sister, DeAnn. I am grateful to God for the beautiful daughters, Angela and Trinity and grandchildren that He has entrusted to me. I am also grateful to my friends, Beverly and Jane, that kept pushing me to publish this work. I love you all.

CHAPTER ONE

BEGINNING TO UNDERSTAND THE MYSTERY OF THE BLINDNESS/ HARDENING OF PART OF ISRAEL

Romans 11:25 For I would not, brethren, that ye should be ignorant of this mystery, lest ye should be wise in your own conceits, that blindness in part is happened to Israel, until the fulness of the Gentiles be come in.

It is important to read who Paul is speaking to. He is speaking to the brethren within this mixed audience in Rome. But, he is very pointed that he is telling the brethren.

Who does Paul define in scripture as the brethren? Let us only use scripture to define scripture:

Romans 9:1 I SAY the truth in Christ, I lie not, my conscience also bearing me witness in the Holy Ghost. 2 That I have great heaviness and continual sorrow in my heart. 3 For I could wish that myself were accursed from Christ for my brethren, my kinsmen according to the flesh. 4 Who are Israelites: to whom pertaineth the adoption, and the glory, and the covenants, and the giving of the law, and the service of God, and the promises;

I realize that Paul goes on to explain more about who are the "children of Abraham", however, Paul makes it clear that "the brethren" are only Israelites. As Paul progresses, after verse 4, much of this is a long prelude is to explain how the religious rulers of the day, the scribes, the Pharisees, are not able to recognizing The Messiah, The Christ. They are the blinded/hardened part of Israel.

This group, that cannot see, that are blind, are the scribes, the Pharisees, the rulers of Jerusalem. Christ clearly speaks to them as we read many times in scripture His "woe to you scribes and Pharisees". Following are the supporting scriptures to understand this group. The scripture is laid out in chronological order:

Isaiah 6:9 And he said, Go, and tell this people, Hear ye indeed, but understand not; and see ye indeed, but perceive not. 10 Make the heart of this people fat, and make their ears heavy, and shut their eyes; lest they see with their eyes; and hear with their ears, and understand with their heart, and convert, and be healed.

Isaiah 44:18 They have not known nor understood: for he hath shut their eyes, that they cannot see: and their hearts, that they cannot understand.

Isaiah 63:17 O LORD, why hast thou made us to err from thy ways, and hardened our heart from thy fear? Return for thy servants' sake, the tribes of thine inheritance.

Matthew 13:10 And the disciples came, and said unto him, Why speakest thou unto them in parables? 11 He answered and said unto them, Because it is given unto you to know the mysteries of the kingdom of heaven, but to them it is not given. 12 For whosoever hath, to him shall be given, and he shall have more abundance: but whosoever hath not, from him shall be taken away even that he hath. 13 Therefore speak I to them in parables; because they seeing see not; and hearing they hear not, neither do they understand. 14 And in them is fulfilled the prophecy of Esaias, which saith By hearing ye shall hear, and shall not understand; and seeing ye shall see, and shall not perceive: 15 For this people's heart is waxed gross, and their ears are dull of hearing, and their eyes they have closed; lest at any time they should see with their eyes, and hear with their ears, and should understand with their heart, and should be converted, and I should heal them. 16 But blessed are your eyes, for they see; and your ears, for they hear. 17 For verily I say unto you, That many prophets and righteous men have desired to see those things which ye see, and have not seen them; and to hear those things which ye hear, and have not heard them.

Mark 4:11 And he said unto them, Unto you it is given to know the mystery of the kingdom of God: but unto them that are without, all these things done in parables: 12 That seeing they may see, and not perceive; and hearing they may hear, and not understand; lest at any time they should be converted, and their sins should be forgiven them.

Luke 8:10 And he said, Unto you it is given to know the mysteries of the kingdom of God: but to others in parables, that seeing they may not see, and hearing they might not understand.

John 12:37 But though he had done so many miracles before them, yet they believed not on him. 38 That the saying of Esaias the prophet might be fulfilled, which he spake, LORD, who hath believed our report? And to whom hath the arm the LORD been revealed? 39 Therefore they could not believe, because that Esaias said again, 40 He hath blinded their eyes, and hardened their heart; that they should not see with their eyes, nor understand with their heart, and be converted, and I should heal them. 41 Nevertheless among the chief rulers also many believed on him; but because of the Pharisees they did not confess him, lest they should be put out of the synagogue: 43 For they loved the praise of men more than the praise of God.

Acts 28:17 And it came to pass, that after three days Paul called the chief of the Jews together: and when they were come together, he said unto them, Men and brethren, though I have committed nothing against the people, or customs of our fathers, yet was delivered prisoner from Jerusalem into the hands of the Romans.......25 And when they agreed not among themselves, they departed, after that Paul had spoken one word, Well spake the Holy Ghost by Esaias the prophet unto our fathers, 26 Saying, Go unto this people, and say, Hearing ye shall hear, and shall not understand; and seeing ye shall see, and not perceive: 27 For the heart of this people is waxed gross, and their ears are dull from hearing, and their eyes have closed; lest they should see with their eyes, and hear with their ears, and understand with their heart, and should be converted, and I should heal them. 28 Be it known therefore unto you, that the salvation of God is sent unto the Gentiles, and that they will hear it.

Romans 11:7 What then? Israel hath not obtained that which he seeketh for; but the election hath obtained it, and the rest were blinded 8 (According as it is written God hath given them the spirit of slumber, eyes that they should not see, and ears that they should not hear;) unto this day. 9 And David saith, Let their table be made a snare, and a trap, and a stumblingblock, and a recompence unto them: 10 Let their eyes be darkened, that they may not see, and bow down their back always. 11 I say the, Have they stumbled that they should fall? God forbid: but rather through their fall salvation is come unto the Gentiles, for to provoke them to jealousy. 12 Now if the fall of them be riches of the world, and the diminishing of them the riches of the Gentiles; how much more their fulness?

Romans 11:25 For I would not, brethren, that ye should be ignorant of this mystery, lest ye be wise in your own conceits, that blindness in part is happened to Israel, until the fulness of the Gentiles be come in. 26 And so all Israel shall be saved: as it is written, There shall come out of Sion the Deliverer, and shall turn away ungodliness from Jacob. 27 For this is my covenant unto them, when I shall take away their sins.

So let's pause here to reflect how we must rightly identify that there are now 4 audiences within the New Testament scriptures. In the Old Testament there were only two audiences: The Jews and The Gentiles. However, with the ministry of Christ, the Jewish audience is divided up into two groups/audiences: 1. the lost sheep of the house of Israel ; 2. the hardened ones/ the scribes/Pharisees/the rulers of Jerusalem,(Jacob); 3. The Gentiles, then when Paul begins to speak to The Church, there is actually 4 within the New Testament. However, we must fully understand these two groups within Israel, because Christ speaks very differently to one and to the other.

Every student of Sacred and Holy Scripture knows that in the Old Testament there are only two audiences: The Jew and The Gentile. Now through the mystery of the hardening of part of

Israel, we now still have the Gentiles but within Israel, there is the part that is hardened and cannot or will not recognize Christ as the Messiah, and the other group, Christ states is, "the lost sheep of the house of Israel," they are the ones as is said of Peter, on this rock Christ has built His Church. Christ has laid the foundation to build His Church.

Then, there comes in The Church, which is throughout the NT, and these different audiences, is a great hurdle to overcome. Do not misunderstand, there is only ONE message of salvation, however, just as Christ, and then Paul, clearly denote, there are three, then four, very specific and different audiences. The third chapter in this book is dedicated to scripture supporting these different audiences.

I am not saying that all scripture is not for everyone. I am not saying that at all. Every word of scripture is for every man and woman. However, just as in the Old Testament everyone knows there are two very specific audiences: 1. The Jew 2.The Gentile. So, it is so in the New Testament, however with the mystery of the hardening of part of Israel, God makes two distinct audiences within Israel now and it will be so until the fullness of the Gentiles come in.

Now back to Paul in Romans:

Romans 11:28 As concerning the gospel, they are enemies for your sakes: but as touching the election, they are beloved for the father's sake.

Romans 11:32 For God hath concluded them all in unbelief, that he might have mercy upon all.

Who is Paul speaking with here? Go back and see, (Romans 11:13 For I speak to you Gentiles), he is speaking to the Gentiles within this whole audience that includes both Jews and Gentiles. He goes back and forth, but he will direct his comments and one has to read carefully, and know when he changes audiences.

Here I must make one very important point:

There is no mystery of the hardening or blindness of the Gentiles from Christ forward. The "pure predestination position", uses Pharaoh to show that God hardens the heart of whom he wills within both groups but this is not so. There is no mystery of the hardening of part of the Gentiles. Repentance is granted to all Gentiles (Acts 11:18) Does this mean all Gentiles will repent? Certainly not! Do not think I am supporting universal salvation because this is not what this means. This means that now the Gentiles are included in the promises and the gift of repentance to eternal life. Each individual must repent and believe and have faith to receive the gift that Christ has made available. Accepting Christ is a personal, individual decision. If you cannot grasp that Pharaoh is used only as an example in scripture, there is no need for you to proceed with reading this book any further…and you may never learn how to fully reconcile the predestined elect to free will. It is your free will to do so. If you stop here, you will be forever stuck in living in the fear of a capricious God who chooses some and not others and His true character of love will stay elusive.

Furthermore, concerning Pharoah, Pharoah is in the OT. If you do a word search for the whole Bible, mystery and mysteries, only come up in the NT. Mystery or mysteries, do not come up at all in the OT. The mysteries in the NT are revealed in

Christ. Mystery comes up 22 times and mysteries comes up 5 times. Many of you may be familiar with these mysteries, for example: The Mystery of God, (the 7th Trumpet); The Mystery of Christ in you; The Mystery of godliness; The Mystery of the Church, (The body of Christ); The Mystery of the Lawless One, (Iniquity, Antichrist); The Mystery of Babylon, The Mystery of the Blindness/The Hardening of part of Israel, and so forth.

In this book, I will be dealing with the Mystery of the Hardening of part of Israel. Many people say that predestination is a mystery. I would say that predestination falls within the mystery of the hardening of part of Israel, so what they say is true in part. The mysteries were revealed in Christ, thus predestination is within a mystery, but the mystery has been revealed in Christ. We have to learn how to read the audiences to understand correctly. Pharoah does not fall into this category. Perhaps Pharoah is just a foreshadowing of the hardening, as we know the OT is Christ concealed and the NT, is Christ revealed. So, please don't let Pharoah confuse this issue.

By the way, believers are considered to be stewards of these mysteries, so I hope you will read them. They are so fascinating and good for your mind, as scripture has the promise to renew your mind.

So, now that we see that there are more audiences in The New Testament, it is important now to see, why God blinded/hardened the hearts of the rulers/the Scribes/the Pharisees. I will list the scriptures that prove that they first "chose evil" over the ways of God, and then the reasons why God allowed their hearts to stay hardened. God never just capriciously hardens an individual's heart. God allows one's heart to become hardened when they choose evil or the things of this world, mammon, or just refuse to love the truth (Jesus is the truth). Concerning Pharaoh, the example from the Gentiles, his sin was that he proclaimed himself to be God.

CHAPTER TWO

WHY GOD ALLOWED THE BLINDNESS/ HARDENING OF PART OF ISRAEL

(I will try to do this in order, to the best of my ability).

1. 1. THEY CHOSE THE THINGS OF THIS WORLD OVER GOD

Isaiah 5:20 Woe unto them that call evil good, and good evil; that put darkness for light, and light for darkness; that put bitter for sweet, and sweet for bitter.

2. THEY HONORED GOD WITH THEIR LIPS BUT NOT THEIR HEARTS.

Isaiah 29:10 For the LORD hath poured out upon you the spirit of deep sleep, and hath closed your eyes: the prophets and your rulers, the seers hath he covered....13 Wherefore the Lord said, Forasmuch as this people draw near me with their mouth, and with their lips do honour me, but have removed their heart far from me, and their fear toward me is taught by precept of men:

Matt 15:7 Ye hypocrites, well did Esaias prophesy of you, saying, 8 This people draweth nigh unto me with their mouth, and honoreth me with their lips; but their heart is far from me.

Mark 7:6-7

3. THE RULERS NEGLECTED THE THINGS OF GOD AND BECAME CORRUPT

Ezekiel 34:1 AND THE word of the LORD came unto me, saying, 2 Son of man, prophecy against the shepherds of Israel, prophecy, and say unto them, Thus saith the LORD GOD unto the shepherds; Woe be to the shepherds of Israel that do feed themselves! Should not the shepherds feed the flocks?

Matt 23:13 But woe unto you scribes and Pharisees, hypocrites! For ye shut up the kingdom of heaven against men: for ye neither go in yourselves, neither suffer ye them that are entering to go in.

(I hope you will read the whole 23rd Chapter).

Matt 23:23 Woe unto you, scribes and Pharisees, hypocrites! For ye pay tithe of mint and anise and cumin, and have omitted the weightier matter of the law, judgment, mercy, and faith: these ought ye to have done, and not to leave the other undone.

4. TO KILL THE HEIR AND GAIN THE INHERITANCE

Matt 21:38 But when the husbandmen say the son, they said among themselves, this is the heir; come, let us kill him, and let us seize on his inheritance.

5.   TO FULFILL THE SCRIPTURE, "THEY HATED ME WITHOUT CAUSE"

John 15:25 But this cometh to pass, that the word might be fulfilled that is written in their law, They hated me without cause.

6.   TO MAKE ISRAEL JEALOUS

Romans 10:19 But I say, did not Israel know? First Moses saith, I will provoke you to jealousy by them that are no people, and by a foolish nation I will anger you.

Duet 32:21 They have moved me to jealousy with that which is not God; they have provoked me to anger with their vanities: and I will move them to jealousy with those which are not my people; I will provoke them to anger with a foolish nation.

7.   TO BRING IN THE GENTILES

Romans 11:11 I say then, Have they stumbled that they should fall? God forbid: but rather through their fall salvation is come unto the Gentiles, for to provoke them to jealousy.

Their hearts were hardened to bring in the Gentiles, for salvation to go out to the ends of the world.

> I hope I have found all of the reasons why God allowed their hearts to be hardened, their eyes to be blind, however there may be additional reasons that I have missed, but I do think I found them all within all of The Bible.

With all of this scripture laid out before you, I hope you now have a good grasp on the mystery of the hardening/blindness of part of Israel and why God allowed this mystery to happen.

Now we will proceed with the scriptures explaining the 4 audiences within the New Testament. Remember, ONE message of salvation: 3 audiences for delivery and then there is also The Church, as the 4th audience.

Let's remember that God had only two audiences within the Old Testament:

1. The Jew
2. The Gentile

THE NEW TESTAMENT AUDIENCES

Audience 1. Within Israel-the hardened part, (Jacob)
Audience 2. Within Israel-(the lost sheep of the house of Israel)
Audience 3. The Gentiles
Audience 4. The Church (the church is spoken to at points and within mixed audiences which indeed makes this subject of reconciling the predestined elect and free will most difficult, especially in the beginning of Ephesians.

CHAPTER THREE

THE FOUR AUDIENCES WITHIN THE NEW TESTAMENT. (THE OT, ONLY HAD TWO, JEW AND GENTILE)

WITHIN ISRAEL - 1. THE HARDENED PART, REFERENCED AS "JACOB" (Romans 11:25)

I have laid out the scriptures explaining one of the audiences: Within Israel, the hardened part, and Christ spoke very harshly to this group in his woe's and in John he even says this to them:

John 8:39 They answered and said unto him, Abraham is our father. Jesus saith unto them, If ye were Abraham's children, ye would do the works of Abraham. 40 But now ye seek to kill me, a man that hath told you the truth, which I have heard of God: this did not Abraham. 41 Ye do the deeds of your father. Then said they to him, We be not born of fornication; we have one Father, even God. 42 Jesus said unto them, If God were your Father, ye would love me: for I proceeded forth and came from God; neither came I of myself, but he sent me. 43 Why do ye not understand my speech? Even because ye cannot hear my word.

I listed previously, the many woe's Christ says to (Jacob), in the book of Matthew, (23).

Importantly, much of the confusion by some regarding some of the passages in The Gospel of John, can be cleared up by understanding that Jesus is speaking with some of the Jews that are hardened. Once one learns to read the different audiences, all of this clears up.

With all of the scriptures listed above, I believe you can get the point that Christ spoke to (Jacob), in parables and Christ never condoned their bad behavior.

Now on to audience number two within Israel:

WITHIN ISRAEL-2. THE LOST SHEEP OF THE HOUSE OF ISRAEL

Matt. 15:24 But he answered and said, I am not sent but unto the lost sheep of the house of Israel.

So let us look at this. It is imperative that we know that there are two audiences within Israel, for if we did not and took this literally, then we may assume that Christ did not come for any Gentiles.

Well, we that know all of the scriptures that state clearly that Christ came to reconcile the whole world and for the salvation of all men. Christ took the sins of the entire world, so we know that Christ indeed came for Gentiles also as the savior thus we must rightly understand these audiences. Christ, is the savior of the world.

What does it mean when Christ said, I was sent only to the lost sheep of the house of Israel. It means that here, Christ, is referring to himself as THE MESSENGER. Some mistakenly think that Christ saying this is that believers are "spiritual sons of Israel". This is not true because the Bible is clear that believers are sons of Abraham. Abraham was before Israel and Abraham was in grace.

So, we have Christ as savior of the world,
Christ as messenger, to the lost sheep of the house of Israel and later, Christ sends Paul, to the Gentiles.

Let us go on and read how Christ speaks to His lost sheep of the house of Israel:

Matt. 5:1 AND SEEING the multitudes, he went up into a : and when he was set, his disciples came unto him: 2 And he opened his mouth, and taught them saying, 3 Blessed are the poor in spirit: for theirs is the kingdom of heaven.

Christ goes on in the passage to continue to bless the lost sheep of the house of Israel, with nine blessings. It is a famous passage.

Matt. 5:17 Think not that I am come to destroy the law, or the prophets: I am not come to destroy, but to fulfil.

So, we can see two very distinct conversations between Christ and these two different parts of Israel. Christ says, "woe" to one audience and He blesses the lost sheep of the house of Israel.

Now it is critical as Christ said, I have come to fulfill the law. Let us ask ourselves, who had the law? The Jews and the Gentiles?

No, only The Jews had the law. How do we know, we will let scripture define scripture:

Romans 9:4 Who are Israelites; to whom pertaineth the adoption, and the glory, and the covenants, and the giving of the law, and the service of God and the promises.

So, Christ fulfills the law for the Old Covenant and for all of Israel. Christ did not have to fulfill the law for The Gentiles because they did not have the law. Christ did become the savior of the whole world and that did include all of mankind, including the Gentiles. However, the fulfilling of the law was very much for Israel. We know from Paul all the through the New Testament that now the sonship has moved into including Gentiles through the gift of grace and righteousness from Christ, but we must understand these audiences and read scripture and not confuse these audiences.

Has The Church now replaced Israel? No emphatically, No! Replacement theology is not correct, and I will deal specifically with this issue in upcoming chapters.

Now back to the audience of the lost sheep of the house of Israel.

So, we have established that Christ said that He was sent only to the lost sheep of the house of Israel. He said that because He fulfilled the law and it was Paul that was sent to the Gentiles. Though Christ interacted with Gentiles, this is what he said about interacting with some Gentiles before their time:

Matt. 15:26 But he answered and said, It is not meet to take the children's bread, and to cast it to the dogs.

(Some translations say, puppies and not dogs, as dogs does seem harsh).

It wasn't until after His resurrection that Christ commanded to go unto all of the world with the good news of eternal life. It was Paul that was chosen by Christ to go to the Gentiles:

Acts 9:15 But the LORD said unto him, Go thy way: for he is a chosen vessel unto me, to bear my name before the Gentiles, and kings, and the children of Israel:

Back to the audience of the lost sheep of the house of Israel…

John 10:27 My sheep hear my voice, and I know them, and they follow me:

John 6:44 No man can come to me, except the Father which hath sent me draw him: and I will raise him up at the last day.

(Many people are confused by this last verse, as they read it to mean all of humanity, both Jew and Gentile. However, Christ is speaking to the hardened part of Israel in this passage, (Jacob).)

Let's now look at this verse:

John 6:64 But there are some of you that believe not. For Jesus know from the beginning who they were that believed not, and who should betray him. 65 And he said, Therefore said I unto you, that no man can come unto me, except it were given unto him of my Father.

Here Christ is explaining, again, as with the speaking in parables, the mystery of the hardening of part of Israel. Christ knew that

God had hardened the hearts of part of Israel and the rest were within the lost sheep of the house of Israel.

How do we know he is not speaking of Jew and Gentiles in John 10:27? Because:

John 10:15 As the Father knoweth me, even so know I the Father: and I lay down my life for the sheep. 16 And other sheep I have, which are not of this fold: them also I must bring, and they shall hear my voice; and there shall be one fold and one shepard.

The other sheep of another fold, are the Gentiles. Jesus states here that they will hear his voice, thus there is no mystery of the hardening of any Gentiles.

The other sheep are The Gentiles. One fold, the lost sheep of the house of Israel, the other fold, The Gentiles, one message of salvation, different folds/audiences, one shepherd, Christ Jesus.

Now if we don't learn to read the audiences than who would be the other fold? Many have actually reached and said, aliens. Well, we know that only man was created in the image of God and only from within mankind can one be called, sons...or daughters, of God.

And to further build the understanding of the different audiences and understand that Christ preached his message of salvation in stages let us look at these scriptures:

Isaiah 40:9 O Zion, that bringest good tidings, get thee up into the high mountain; O Jerusalem, that bringest good tidings, lift up thy voice with strength; lift it up be not afraid; say unto the cities of Judah, Behold your God! 10 Behold, the LORD GOD will come with strong hand, and his arm shall rule for him: behold, his reward is with him and his work before him.

Acts 14:46 Then Paul and Barnabas waxed bold, and said, It was necessary that the word of God should first have been spoken to you: but seeing ye put it from you, and judge yourselves unworthy of everlasting life, lo, we turn to the Gentiles. 47 For so hath the LORD commanded us, saying, I have set thee to be a light of the Gentiles, that thou shouldest be for salvation unto the ends of the earth.

Acts 10:34 Then Peter opened his mouth, and said, Of a truth I perceive that God is no respecter of persons. 35 But in every nation he that feareth him, and worketh righteousness, is accepted with him.

Luke 24:47 And that repentance and remission of sins should be preached in his name among all nations, beginning at Jerusalem.

The messianic Jews still say, "To the Jew first". One message of salvation, different audiences.

Now the Gentiles are included but they were not until "It was finished" and Christ had fulfilled the law.

Acts 11:17 Forasmuch then as God gave them the like gift as he did unto us, who believed on the LORD Jesus Christ; what was I, that I could withstand God? 18 when they heard these things, they held their peace, and glorified God, saying, then hath God also to the Gentiles granted repentance unto life.

In your understanding of scripture, do not underestimate the effect that the mystery of the hardening of part of Israel had on all of the people of Israel. The learned people, the scribes, the lawyers, the rulers of Jerusalem did not/could not recognize Christ. All of the rulers of Jerusalem, that knew the scriptures that should have recognized Christ/God, did not, and then the fact that they were pursuing the Church and killing the Christians, do not under estimate this fact. It had to have been extremely difficult on the common man and woman, and during a difficult time.

It is now possible for the Gentiles to believe in Christ. Will all believe? No, it depends on the individual, and we know from within scripture God speaks of the call to repentance and many never repent and believe.

Notice that nowhere in scripture, is there "a mystery of the hardening of the Gentiles". Pharoah is just an example that Paul uses. Pharoah is in the OT, before the mysteries that were revealed in Christ. Pharoah is a Gentile and cannot be with the mystery of the hardening of part of Israel, as Pharoah was not within Israel.

Now, to the audience of The Gentiles:

3. THE AUDIENCE OF THE GENTILES

Romans 1:16 For I am not ashamed of the gospel of Christ: for it is the power of God unto salvation to every one that believeth; to the Jew first, and also to the Greek. 17 For therein is the righteousness of God revealed from faith to faith: as it is written, The just shall live by faith.

Romans 2:14 For when the Gentiles, which have not the law, do by nature the things contained in the law, these, having not the law, are a law unto themselves. 15 Which shew the work of the law written in their hearts, their conscience also bearing witness, and their thoughts the mean while accusing or else excusing one another;)

Romans 9:25 As he saith also in Osee, I will call them my people, which were not my people; and her beloved, which was not beloved. 26 And it shall come to pass, that in the place where it was said unto the, Ye are not my people; there shall be called the children of the living God.

Most definitely different audiences, but let us just stop and meditate on that fact that believers of all nations, God calls us His beloved. God first called Christ, His beloved Son, as Christ is preeminent in everything, and now also, we are beloved.

Romans 11:13 For I speak to you Gentiles, inasmuch as I am the apostle of the Gentiles, I magnify mine office:

Paul addressing a mixed audience in the Book of Romans and he is very pointed as to which audience he is speaking to and when. If we read carefully, Paul tells us like in 11:13 that he has now changed audiences.

In Ephesians Paul further explains

It is here in Ephesians that Paul finally addresses the Gentiles within this mixed audience:

Ephesians 2:11 Wherefore remember that ye being in time past Gentiles in the flesh, who are called Uncircumcision by that which is called the Circumcision in the flesh made by hands; 12 That at that time ye were without Christ, being aliens from the commonwealth of Israel, and strangers from the covenants of promise, having no hope, and without God in the world: 13 But now in Christ ye who sometimes were far off are made nigh by the blood of Christ.

Ephesians 2:19 Now therefore ye are no more strangers and foreigners, but fellowcitizens with the saints, and of the household of God;

Let us stop and take note of what Paul said:
Saints
Fellow citizens

Ephesians 3:6 That the Gentiles should be fellowheirs, and of the same body, and partakers of his promise in Christ by the gospel:

Acts 14:27 And when they were come, and had gathered the church together, they rehearsed all that God had done with them, and how he had opened the door of faith unto the Gentiles.

Christ explains the audiences in an amazing passage in Luke:

Luke 14:16 Then said he unto him, A certain man made a great supper, and bade many: 17 And sent his servant at supper time to say to them that were bidden, Come; for all things are now ready. 18 And they all with one consent began to make excuse. The first said unto him, I have bought a piece of ground, and I must needs go and see it: I pray thee have me excused. 19 And another said, I have bought five yoke of oxen, and I go to prove them: I pray thee have me excused. 20 And another said, I have married a wife, and therefore I cannot come. 21 So that the servant came, and shewed his lord these things. Then the master of the house being angry said to his servant, Go out quickly into the streets and lanes of the city, and bring in hither the poor, and the maimed and the halt, and the blind. 22 And the servant said, Lord, it is done as thou has commanded, and yet there is room. 23 And the lord said unto the servant, Go out into the highways and hedges, and compel them to come in, that my house may be filled. 24 For I say unto you, That none of those men which were bidden shall taste of my supper.

So, clearly, the scribes and Pharisees are the first audience invited. Then, the invitation goes out to the lost sheep of the house of Israel. The last invitation goes out to The Gentiles. (Side note, it is most interesting that it reads like the scribes and Pharisees, (the group, Jacob) will not be at the wedding supper, but I may be wrong).

"To the Jew first, the two groups, and then to The Gentile".

4.Audience is The Church

Now that we understand how to read the distinct audiences, we can pick up when the church is being spoken to as well.

Before we proceed with other issues within this mystery of the hardening of part of Israel, lets look at some scriptures that may be telling of what happens to this group, Jacob, as God delights in mercy.

Romans 11:26 And so all Israel shall be saved: as it is written, There shall come out of Sion the Deliverer, and shall turn away ungodliness from Jacob:

How does the Deliverer banish ungodliness from Jacob?

Jeremiah 30:7 Alas! For that day is great, so that none is like it: it is even the time of Jacob's trouble; but he shall be saved out of it.

Jeremiah 46:28 Fear thou not, O Jacob my servant, saith the LORD: for I am with thee; for I will make a full end of all the nations whither I have driven thee: but I will not make a full end of thee, but correct thee in measure; yet will I not leave thee wholly unpunished.

Isaiah 27:6 He shall cause them that come of Jacob to take root: Israel shall blossom and bud, and fill the face of the world with fruit.

Many believe the time of "Jacob's distress" is the 7 years of tribulation, where Jacob is finally the witnesses that they were supposed to be when Christ came to earth. Within this group, will be the 144,000 and they will witness to Christ and save a multitude, no man can number (Rev. 7:9-14).

On your own, it is good to do a "word search" for Jacob. One must distinguish between when scripture is talking about the individual, Jacob, or the group of the hardened, Jacob.

> What Does Scripture Say About Why God Chooses?

> Let us define scripture by scripture.

THE CHOSEN PEOPLE-The Jews of the Old Testament

Why are they Chosen?

Deut. 14:2 For thou art an holy people unto the LORD thy God, and the LORD hath chosen thee to be a peculiar people unto himself, above all the nations that are upon the earth.

1 Kings 8:60 That all the people of the earth may know that the LORD is God, and that there is none else.

1. To make known that there is One God.

Isaiah 43:10 Ye are my witnesses, saith the LORD, and my servant whom I have chosen: that ye may know and believe me, and understand that I am he: before me there was no God formed, neither shall there be after me. 11 I, even I, am the LORD and beside me there is no saviour.

2. They are witnesses to all of the peoples of the earth.

Isaiah 49:6 And he said, It is a light thing that thou shouldest be my servant to raise up the tribes of Jacob, and to restore the preserved of Israel: I will also give thee for a light to the Gentiles, that thou mayest be my salvation unto the end of the earth.

3. They are chosen to be a light to all nations, that God's salvation may reach the end of the earth.

God chooses to make witnesses/facilitators/instruments to go and include all of the peoples of the earth. God never makes choice to exclude anyone. God makes choice of the messengers to be a light to all of the nations to the end of the earth. They are chosen to be inclusive not exclusive. The entire Gentile world knows and is okay with the fact that the Jewish people are the chosen people.

Now let us look at The New Testament and see what scripture tells us about when God's again, makes choice.

CHAPTER FOUR

WHO ARE THE ELECT AND THE PREDESTINED ELECT?

Christ says this and it is very interesting:

Matt 13:33 Another parable He spoke to them: "The kingdom of heaven is like leaven, which a woman took and hid in three measures of meal till it was all leavened."

1. THE FIRST ELECT

IT IS IMPORTANT TO INTERJECT HERE CONCERNING THE FIRST MENTION OF ELECT, IT IS OF CHRIST BECAUSE, CHRIST IS PREIMINANT IN EVERYTHING!

Isaiah 42:1 BEHOLD MY servant, whom I uphold; mine elect, in whom my soul delighteth; I have put my spirit upon him: he shall bring forth judgment to the Gentiles.

THE SECOND MENTION OF ELECT

Isaiah 45:4 For Jacob my servant's sake, and Israel mine elect, I have called thee by thy name: I have surnamed thee, though thou hast not known me.

This is what we know concerning the first election:

2. THE FIRST ELECTION:

Romans 9:11 (For the children being not yet born, neither having done any good or evil, that the purpose of God according to election might stand, not of works, but of him that calleth;)

The first election reads to be Jacob, the person.

Now enters the "predestined elect". There is no mention in the OT concerning "predestined". "Elect" is mentioned in the OT.

3. THE PREDESTINED ELECT, (THE LOST SHEEP OF THE HOUSE OF ISRAEL)

4. THE PREDESTINED ELECT IN THE BOOK OF REVELATION (THE 144,000 OF THE TWELVE TRIBES OF ISRAEL)

The predestined elect, as we have laid out by using scripture to explain scripture are "the lost sheep of the house of Israel" AND the 144,000 in Revelation.

How do we know that they are the same group? They are the only ones within scripture, who's names are written in the Lambs Book of Life before the foundation of the world.

Within the following chapters, I will go into the different "times" that individuals names are written into The Lambs Book of Life. But for now, we will let scripture tell us about the predestined elect.

Romans 8:29 For whom he did foreknow, he also did predestinate to be conformed to the image of his Son, that he might be the firstborn among many brethren.

Again, does it say to exclude anyone? No, it says to be the first-born among many brethren.

Romans 8:30 Moreover whom he did predestinate, them he also called: and whom he called, them he also justified: and whom he justified, them he also glorified.

Romans 11:7 What then? Israel hath not obtained that which he seeketh for; but the election hath obtained it, and the rest were blinded.

Recap: The lost sheep of the house of Israel, obtained it. Jacob the group was blind. Then the message went out to the Gentiles.

Ephesians is a most beautiful love letter to believers. As we read the audiences, Paul does not address the Gentiles until (Ephesians 2:11). In Paul's address to the Gentiles, he says this:

Ephesians 2:19 Now therefore ye are no more strangers and foreigners, but fellowcitizens with the saints, and the household of God.

The lost sheep of the house of Israel are the first group of the predestined elect.

Ephesians 1:11 In whom also we have obtained and inheritance, being predestinated according to the purpose of him who worketh all things after the counsel of his own will.

The second group of the predestined elect are the 144,000 in the book of Revelation.

Rev. 7:4 And I heard the number of them which were sealed: and there were sealed and hundred and forty and four thousand of all the tribes of Israel.

Rev. 13:8 And all that dwell upon the earth shall worship him, whose names are not written in the book of life of the Lamb slain from the foundation of the world.

Why are there these two groups the predestined elect, who's names are written in the Lambs book of life before the foundation of the world, and what do they do?

They are describes in scripture, as "first fruits", the foundation after Christ, to the building of The Church and believers in Revelation.

James 1:18 Of his own will begat he us with the word of truth, that we should be a kind of first-fruits of his creatures.

Romans 11:16 For if the firstfruit be holy, the lump also holy: and if the root be holy, so are the branches.

John 15:16 Ye have not chosen me, but I have chosen you, and ordained you, that ye should go and bring forth fruit, and that your fruit should remain: ...

Romans 8:23 and not only they, but ourselves also, which have the firstfruits of the Spirit...

Rev. 14:4 These are they which were not defiled with women; for they are virgins. These are they which follow the Lamb whithersoever he goeth. These were redeemed from among men, being the firstfruits unto God and the Lamb.

CHAPTER FIVE

GOD CALLS TO ALL

Romans 9:24 Even us, whom he hath called, not of the Jews only, but also of the Gentiles? 25 As he saith also in Osee, I will call them my people, which were not my people; and her beloved. 26 And it shall come to pass, that in the place where it was said unto them, Ye are not my people; there shall they be called the children of the living God.

Gentiles are called to by God, they are beloved and can be sons of the living God. This is not saying universal salvation for all of the Gentiles. Christianity is not a collective salvation, it is an individual salvation. One must have faith that Christ is the Lord, the Son of God, and He was raised from the dead. Each individual must have faith and believe themselves.

1 Cor. 1:24 But unto them which are called, both Jews and Greeks, Christ the power of God, and the wisdom of God.

Isaiah 55:1 HO, EVERY one that thirsteth, come ye to the waters, and he that hath no money; come ye, buy, and eat; yea, come, buy wine and milk without money and without price. 2 Wherefore do ye spend money for that which is not bread? And your labour for that which satisfieth not? Hearken diligently unto me, and eat ye that which is good, and let your soul delight itself in fatness. 3 Incline your ear, and come unto me: hear, and your soul shall live; and I will make an everlasting covenant with you, even the sure mercies of David. 4 Behold, I have given him for a witness to the people, a leader and commander to the people. 5 Behold, thou shalt call a nation that knowest not, and nations that knew not thee shall run unto thee because of the LORD they God, and for the Holy One of Israel; for he hath glorified thee. 6 Seek ye the LORD while he may be found, call ye upon him while he is near:

Thank you Lord for your steadfast love for all of mankind.

We already established in early chapters that repentance was granted to the Gentiles and also that there is no mystery of the hardening of any Gentiles from the birth of Christ on.

Matt. 28:19 Go ye therefore, and teach all nations, baptizing them in the name of the Father, and of the Son, and of the Holy Ghost:

Before we talk about The Lambs Book of Life, one should be aware that there are many books spoken of throughout scripture. The book of the living, everyone is written in this book. There are the Books of Remembrance. There are the books of people actions that are opened in Revelation 20. There are many different books, however the next chapter is concerning The Lambs Book of Life.

Within the subject of a call, or a calling, there is also a call regarding one's vocation.

CHAPTER SIX

AT HOW MANY DIFFERENT "TIMES", ARE NAMES WRITTEN INTO THE LAMBS BOOK OF LIFE (THE BOOK OF THE RIGHTEOUS)?

We have well established that the predestined elect were written into the Lambs Book of Life before the foundation of the world.

Is this the only time that writing of names is discussed in scripture? No, it is not. King David says this about the people in the Old Testament:

Psalms 69:28 Let them be blotted out of the book of the living, and not be written with the righteous.

So, David is living when he wrote the above scripture and says that it is possible for the living to be written in with the righteous.

These people obviously, were not written in before the foundation of the world. Look at the wonderful reason why...

We find the explanation in 1 Cor. And in Hebrews.

1 Cor. 15:20 But every man in his own order: Christ the firstfruits; afterward they that are Christ's at his coming.

Who are those who have fallen asleep? I do know that all of the Kings of Judah and Israel, it is written that when they died, they slept with their fathers. I do not know for sure if this pertains to all of the peoples of the earth but nevertheless, let us read on in scripture as to what happened after Christ died and was buried:

1 Pet. 3:18 For Christ also hath once suffered for sins, the just for the unjust, that he might bring us to God, being put to death in the flesh, but quickened by the Spirit: 19 By which also he went and preached unto the spirits in prison.

Eph 4:8 Wherefore he saith, When he ascended up on high, he led captivity captive, and gave gifts to men. 9 (Now that he ascended, what is it but that he also descended first into the lower parts of the earth? 10 He that descended is the same also that ascended up far above all heavens, that he might fill all things.)

Psalms 68:18 Thou hast ascended on high, thou hast led captivity captive: thou hast received gifts for men; yea, for the rebellious also, that the LORD GOD might dwell among them.

As Christ ascended he led captivity captive. Were these captives the spirits in prison below the earth? Did he ascend with the ones who believed? Were their names enrolled among the righteous in heaven?

Ok, so back to Christ as the first fruits of those who have fallen asleep.

As we must keep as our focus through all of The Bible, Christ is preeminent in everything. Everything.

Let us read now how this effects the times that persons names can be written into The Lambs Book of Life/Righteous.

Let us remember, when we read, we must also keep in mind the audience to which it is written. (All scripture is for everyone, but knowing how to read the audiences clarifies much confusion).

Hebrews 11:39 And these all, having obtained a good report through faith, received not the promise: 40 God having provided some better thing for us, that they without us, should not be made perfect.

Apart from whom? The predestined elect. The lost sheep of the house of Israel.

Perfect how? Perfect in Christ, by Christ.

At what time are the Gentiles written in? They are written in as each one believes. Yes, there is a lot of writing going on in heaven.

In Romans it refers to the spirit of adoption, but adoption as a record, or the sealing of the spirit?

Rev. 20:15 And whosoever was not found written in the book of life was cast into the lake of fire.

There's that pesty whosoever again…

Rev. 21:27 And there shall in no wise enter into it any thing that defileth, neither whatsoever worketh abomination, or maketh a lie: but they which are written in the Lamb's book of life.

CHAPTER SEVEN

THE EXISTENCE OF THE AGENT OF FREE WILL

If you learn anything from this book, I hope you learn that free will of mankind and free will of the angels, exist only within the parameters of God's PURPOSE.

James 1:13 Let no man say when he is tempted, I am tempted of God: for God cannot be tempted with evil, neither tempteth he any man: 14 But every man is tempted, when he is drawn away of his own lust, and enticed. 15 then when lust hath conceived, it bringeth forth sin: and sin, when it is finished, bringeth forth death.

Genesis 2:16 And the LORD GOD commanded the man, saying, Of every tree of the garden thou mayest freely eat: 17 But of the tree of the knowledge of good and evil, thou shalt not eat of it: for in the day that thou eatest thereof thou shalt surely die.

Genesis 4:7 If thou doest well, shalt thou not be accepted? And if thou doest not well, sin lieth at the door. And unto thee shall be his desire, and thou shalt rule over him.

Matt 15:19 For out of the heart proceed evil thoughts, murders, adulteries, fornications, thefts, false witness, blasphemies. 20 These are the things which defile a man: but to eat with unwashed hands defileth not a man.

Hebrews 3:10 Wherefore I was grieved with that generation, and said, They do always err in their heart; and they have not known my ways.

Jeremiah 3:17…neither shall they walk any more after the imagination of their evil heart.

Isaiah 30:1 WOE TO the rebellious children, saith the LORD, that take counsel, but not of me; and that cover with a covering, but not of my spirit, that they may add sin to sin:

GOD'S WILL

Isaiah 53:6 All we like sheep have gone astray; we have turned every one to his own way; and the LORD hath laid on him the iniquity of us all.

Matt 6:10 Thy kingdom come. Thy will be done in earth, as it is in heaven.

John 9:31 Now we know that God heareth not sinners: but if any man be a worshipper of God, and doeth his will, him he heareth.

James 1:18 Of his own will begat he us with the word of truth, that we should be a kind of firstfruits of his creatures.

CHRIST'S FREE WILL

Isaiah 7:14 Therefore the LORD himself shall give you a sign; Behold, a virgin shall conceive, and bear a son, and shall call his name Immanuel. 15 Butter and honey shall he eat, that he may know to refuse the evil, and choose the good.

Matt. 26:39 And he went a little further, and fell on his face, and prayed, saying, O my Father, if it be possible, let this cup pass from me: nevertheless not as I will, but as thou wilt.

Mark 14:36 And he said, Abba, Father, all things are possible unto thee; take away this cup from me: nevertheless not what I will, but what thou wilt.

Luke 22:42 Saying, Father, if thou be willing, remove this cup from me: nevertheless not my will, but thine, be done.

MAN'S FREE WILL

John 1:13 Which were born, not of blood, nor of the will of flesh, nor of the will of man, but of God.

Romans 9:16 So then it is not of him that willeth, nor of him that runneth, but of God that sheweth mercy.

Isaiah 53:6 All we like sheep have gone astray; we have turned every one to his own way; and the LORD hath laid on him the iniquity of us all.

John 8:44 Ye are of your father the devil, and the lusts of your father ye will do....

Deut. 30:19 I call heaven and earth to record this day against you, that I have set before you life and death, blessing and cursing: therefore choose life, that both thou and thy seed may live.

Isaiah 58:13 If thou turn away thy foot from the sabbath, from doing thy pleasure on my holy day; and call the sabbath a delight, and holy of the LORD, honourable; and shalt honour him, not doing thine own ways, nor finding thine own pleasure, nor speaking thine own words:

Isaiah 65:12 Therefore will I number you to the sword, and ye shall all bow down to the slaughter: because when I called, ye did not answer; when I spake, ye did not hear; but did evil before mine eyes, and did choose that wherein I delighted not,

Isaiah 66:3 ...Yea, they have chosen their own ways, and their sould delighteth in their abominations.

Daniel 11:3 And a mighty king shall stand up, that shall rule with great dominion, and do according to his will.

Daniel 11:16 But he that cometh against him shall do according to his own will, and none shall stand before him: and he shall stand in the glorious land, which by his hand shall be consumed.

Daniel 11:36 And the king shall do according to his will; and shall exalt himself, and magnify himself above every god, and shall speak marvellous thing against the God of gods, and shall prosper till the indignation be accomplished: for that that is determined shall be done.

SATAN'S FREE WILL

Ezekiel 28:15 Thou wast perfect in thy ways from the day that thou wast created, till iniquity was found in thee.

And Satan's great "I will", count them 5:

Isaiah 14:13 For thou hast said in thine heart, I will ascend into heaven, I will exalt my throne above the stars of God: I will sit also upon the mount of the congregation, in the sides of the north: 14 I will ascend above the heights of the clouds; I will be like the most High.

2 Tim. 2:26 And that they may recover themselves out of the snare of the devil, who are taken captive by him at his will.

The scripture proof of free will is there, now let us reconcile this with the full and complete Sovereignty of God.

CHAPTER EIGHT

GOD'S SOVEREIGN WILL AND HIS DESIGN FOR THIS UNIVERSE

God is indeed Sovereign in the universe. There is nothing outside of His control and there is nothing that He cannot do.

One must not confuse God's Sovereignty with God's purposeful design of His universe. It is God's will that mankind and the angels have free will. The agent of free will does not in any way diminish God's Sovereignty.

Free will can operate in God's universe because it is God's purpose that will always be accomplished. Man and angels are not always obedient but that will not thwart God's purpose. It is God's purpose that will always be fulfilled. Let us examine the scriptures.

Isaiah 46:9 Remember the former things of old: for I am God, and there is none else; I am God, and there is none like me, 10 Declaring the end from the beginning, and from ancient times the things that are not yet done, saying, My counsel shall stand, and I will do all my pleasure: 11 Calling a ravenous bird from the east, the man that executeth my counsel from a far country:

yea, I have spoken it, I will also bring it to pass; I have purposed it, I will also do it.

Purpose.

Isaiah 14:24 The LORD of hosts hath sworn, saying, Surely as I have thought, so shall it come to pass; and as I have purposed, so shall it stand...26 This is the purpose that is purposed upon the whole earth: and this is the hand that is stretched out upon all the nations. 27 For the LORD of hosts hath purposed, and who shall disannul it? and his hand is stretched out, and who shall turn it back?

Isaiah 19:12; 23:9; Jeremiah 4:28; 26:3; 36:3; 49:30; 50:45;

Jeremiah 51:29 And the land shall tremble and sorrow: for every purpose of the LORD shall be preformed against Babylon, to make the land of Babylon a desolation without inhabitant.

Eph. 1:11 In whom also we have obtained an inheritance, being predestinated according to the purpose of him who worketh all things after the counsel of his own will.

Eph. 3:11 According to the eternal purpose which he purposed in Christ Jesus our Lord.

Esther 4:14 For if thou altogether holdest thy peace at this time, then shall there enlargement and deliverance arise to the Jews from another place; but thou and thy father's house shall be destroyed: and who knoweth whether thou art come to the kingdom for such a time as this?

God's purpose will always be fulfilled. Free will operates within God's purpose. One must pray and align their will to God's will.

Romans 8:28 And we know that all things work together for good to them that love God, to them who are called according to his purpose.

Ecclesiastes 3:11 TO EVERY thing there is a season, and a time to every purpose under heaven.

2 Tim. 1:9 Who hath saved us, and called us with an holy calling, not according to our works, but according to his own purpose and grace, which was given us in Christ Jesus before the world began.

1 John 3:8 He that committeth sin is of the devil; for the devil sinneth from the beginning. For this purpose the Son of God was manifested, that he might destroy the works of the devil.

MAN'S FREE WILL AND THE ANGELS FREE WILL OPERATE WITHIN THE PARAMETERS OF GOD'S PURPOSE

GOD'S PURPOSEFUL DESIGN OF THIS WORLD WITHIN HIS SOVERIEGTY

Romans 11:32 For God hath concluded them all in unbelief, that he might have mercy upon all.

Gal. 3:22 But the scripture hath concluded all under sin, that the promise by faith of Jesus Christ, might be given to them that believe.

God consigned this world to sin. God has left this world in a fallen state that through His eternal purpose of sending His Son in grace, he may have mercy on all.

Isaiah 55:7 Let the wicked forsake his way, and the unrighteous man his thoughts: and let him return unto the LORD, and he will have mercy upon him; and to our God, for he will abundantly pardon. 8 For my thoughts are not your thoughts, neither are your way my ways, saith the LORD.

Many quote the above scripture in Isaiah to try to convince some, that one can never understand the LORD. However, they erroneously leave out verse 7, which would keep the verse in context pertaining that God would have mercy on people that we may not. People sometimes see sinners and want to exact punishment, especially if they are thinking they are totally depraved. God is saying that he is a merciful God and delights in mercy. We must give Christ his full sacrifice, that he took the sins of the world, the iniquity of us all, the punishment and the curse.

God would indeed show mercy, where man's heart may want to extract the punishment.

Now that we have let scripture define who are the predestined elect, and how free will can exist with the two groups of the predestinated elect. I would be remiss if I did not give a list of scripture that show that salvation is available to all that believe. Not all will hear with faith, but Christ took the sins of the whole world and made salvation AVAILABLE TO ALL WHO HAVE FAITH AND BELIEVE. It is an individual relationship, an individual choice.

CHAPTER NINE

FOR THE GRACE OF GOD HAS APPEARED FOR THE SALVATION OF ALL MEN.

Titus 2:11 For the grace of God that bringeth salvation hath appeared to all men.

1 Tim. 2:3 For this is good and acceptable in the sight of God our Saviour; 4 Who will have all men to saved, and to come unto the knowledge of the truth. 5 For there is one God, and one mediator between God and men, the man Christ Jesus; 6 Who gave himself a ransom for all, to be testified in due time.

1 Pet. 3:18 For Christ also hath once suffered for sins, the just and the unjust, that he might bring us to God, being put to death in the flesh, but quickened by the Spirit:

2 Cor. 5:14 For the love of Christ constraineth us; because we thus judge, that if one died for all, then were all dead. 15 And that he died for all that they which live should not henceforth live unto themselves, but unto him which died for them, and rose again.

2 Cor. 5:19 To wit, that God was in Christ, reconciling the world unto himself, not imputing their trespasses unto them; and hath committed unto us the word of reconciliation.

1 John 2:2 And he is the propitiation for our sins: and not for ours only, but also for the sins of the whole world.

John 1:29 The next day John seeth Jesus coming unto him, and saith, Behold the Lamb of God, which taketh away the sin of the world.

Acts 17:30 And the times of this ignorance God winked at; but now commandeth all men every where to repent.

2 Pet. 3:9 The LORD is not slack concerning his promise, as some men count slackness; but is longsuffering to us-ward, not willing that any should perish, but that all should come to repentance.

John 4:42 And said unto the woman, Now we believe, not because of thy saying: for we have heard him ourselves, and know that this is indeed the Christ, the Saviour of the world.

Hebrews 2:9 But we see Jesus, who was made a little lower than the angels for the suffering of death, crowned with glory and honour; that he by the grace of God should taste death for every man.

Romans 2:11 For there is no respect of persons with God.

Eph. 6:9 And, ye masters, go the same things unto them, forbearing threatening: knowing that your Master also is in heaven; neither is there respect of persons with him.

Acts 10:34 Then Peter opened his mouth, and said, Of a truth I perceive that God is no respecter of persons:

John 3:16 For God so loved the world, that he gave his only begotten Son, that whosoever believeth in him should not perish, but have everlasting life.

Whosoever can be saved, not just his elect or his predestined elect.

CHAPTER TEN

THE RIGHTEOUS SCEPTRE OF JUDAH

Numbers 24: I shall see him, but not now: I shall behold him, but not nigh: there shall come a Star out of Jacob, and a Sceptre shall rise out of Israel, and shall smite the corners of Moab, and destroy all the children of Sheth.

Genesis 49:10 The sceptre shall not depart from Judah, nor a lawgiver from between his feet, until Shiloh come; and unto him shall the gathering of the people be.

Hebrews 2:8 Thou hast put all things in subjection under his feet. For in that he put all in subjection under him, he left nothing that is not put under him. But now we see not yet all thing put under him.

1 Cor. 15:23 But every man in his own order: Christ the firstfruits; afterward they that are Christ's at his coming. 24 Then cometh the end, when he shall have delivered up the kingdom of God, even the Father; when he shall have put down all rule and all authority and power. 25 For he must reign, till he hath put all enemies under his feet. 26 The last enemy that shall be destroyed is death. 27 For he hath put all things under his feet. But when he saith all things are put under him, it is

manifest that he is excepted, which did put all things under him. 28 And when all things shall be subdued unto him, then shall the Son also himself be subject unto him that put all things under him, that God may be all in all.

Is the above scripture, the telling of the process of the passing away of free will?

CHAPTER ELEVEN

FATALISM IS NOT A GODLY CHARACTERISTIC

Hebrew 11:6 But without faith it is impossible to please him: for he that cometh to God must believe that he is, and that he is a rewarder of them that diligently seek him.

Mark 1:37 And when they found him, they said unto him, All men seek for thee.

Matt. 19:26 But Jesus beheld them, and said unto them, With men this is impossible; but with God all things are possible.

Mark 9:23 Jesus said unto him, If thou canst believe, all things are possible to him that believeth.

Philippians 4:13 I can do all things through Christ which strengtheneth me.

CHAPTER TWELVE

GOD IS LOVE

1 John 4:8 He that loveth not knoweth not God; for God is love.

1 John 4:16 And we have known and believed the love that God hath to us. God is love; and he that dwelleth in love dwelleth in God, and God in him.

CHAPTER THIRTEEN
THE "SUBJECT" OF PREDESTINATION

The "subject" of predestination is totally different than the two specific groups of the predestined elect. The subject of predestination is about the purpose that God designed for your life. I have heard Psychologists report something like that there is a difference between people that are depressed and people that are despairing or in despair. People in despair feel their life has no purpose and do not understand why they were born.

PURPOSE: God gives everyone a purpose or many purposes, for why they were created. The story in the Bible that talks about the talents given, I believe it pertains to money, however, we could also look at this as talents given by the Lord. Our talents would be something that we are good at, gifts, and things like we like to do. Some people find their purpose, as Ester recognized hers when presented. Some people, on the other hand, for whatever reason, may not find it, or may find it and not fulfill it.

PATH/PLAN: God has a plan designed for every life. To find this plan, we have to find our path and stay on this path. Scripture tells us over and over to read The Bible to make sure we are keeping our feet to our path. In my personal opinion, I believe that if we get off of our path, God will give us intersections that we can get back on our path. I have experienced this and recognized it as such. Through prayer, reading the Bible, following prompting of The Holy Spirit, we keep aligning our will with God's will.

SALVATION/ETERNAL LIFE WITH OUR CREATOR: Christ took the sins of the world and made salvation AVAILABLE to whosoever would believe and have faith. God desires all men to come to salvation, thus God it is God's will that all find eternal life with Him through faith in His Son.

Each individual with the above issues, may find one, may find two, may find all three or any combination therein. It is critically important as Christians, we help people through this life and influence our cultural for people to have a purposeful life.

CONCLUDING STATEMENTS

I hope I have successfully laid out scriptures for you to see this reconciliation for yourself. I hope that you see now that God is love. That we can understand God for Christ said:

John 14:9 Jesus saith unto him, Have I been so long time with you, and yet hast thou not known me, Philip? he that hath seen me hath seen the Father; and how sayest thou then, Shew us the Father?

We can understand God in the person of Christ. No, we do not fully comprehend the Creator of this amazing universe, but through the love of God, the grace of Jesus and the fellowship of the Holy Spirit, we know everything we need to know about the family relationship God desires to have with us. God's love story to us is written in the language of family. The family was the first institution that God created and is so critically important on this earth. God, the Father (Abba-Daddy), Yeshua (Jesus) the Son, and believers become sons and daughters. Everything God writes is of the love of family. Our love and our life of worship and service to Him is all that we have to offer, Creator God. He does not invade our will. He does not want our love out of compulsion, but wants us to love Him of our own free will and become part of his family.

I hope one can now move fully from the understanding of a Sovereign God into a love relationship with a loving Heavenly Father, that is love itself.

Blessings in Christ.

M.E. Jacob

ABOUT THE AUTHOR

She grew up in a family with the extended family having four Presbyterian Ministers. How to reconcile Predestination and Free Will was a common topic at family gatherings, family reunions, the dinner table and causual discussions.

Printed in the United States
by Baker & Taylor Publisher Services